LOVE SONGS OF
ASIA

*

rendered by
POWYS MATHERS

*

LONDON
THE PUSHKIN PRESS
10 NOTTINGHAM PLACE, W.I.

First published in this form in 1944

PRINTED IN GREAT BRITAIN BY THE CHISWICK PRESS LTD.
NEW SOUTHGATE, LONDON, N.11.

CONTENTS

FOREWORD

THIS COLLECTION contains *Black Marigolds*, 1919, and selections from the poems in *Coloured Stars*, 1918, and *The Garden of Bright Waters*, 1920, all published by Basil Blackwell.

These were my husband's earliest publications: the first two volumes were completed during the last war and most of the work on the third was done before 1918.

In his Foreword to *Black Marigolds* he says:"My rendering was finished in two or three sessions on a box by the stove in hutments and I have not cared to risk a discrepancy of moods in more luxurious minutes and places." His attitude would be the same to the other poems here reprinted: slight verbal changes he might have made, but he deplored a poet in middle age tinkering with his young work.

But one defect he would, emphatically, have remedied: he would have enlisted the help of experts, and transliterated all proper names in accordance with the conventions of English scholarship. At the time of publication he was only interested in the poetic angle: mostly he copied the French spelling because for years he had explored the Orient in that language. But French transliteration is determined by French phonetics.

The result of this indifference is, as he said himself, a "distressingly unscholarly hotch-potch." Ordinarily I should myself have made the necessary contacts, but—in the fifth year of the World War, with over-pressure in every department of work—it has seemed best to give the selections from these volumes just as they were presented in the Great War a quarter of a century ago.

"I am hoping," he says in his note to *The Garden of Bright Waters*, "that some people will look on this collection primarily as a book of poems." He was not disappointed; and I trust that these songs will be received now, as they were then, with gladness for their poetic grace, the vigour and freshness of their imagery, the various richness of their colour.

This note may best conclude with the first few lines of the Foreword to *Coloured Stars*.

"There is an opportunity of knowing in brilliant English translations much of the poetry of China and Japan, of India and Persia; and Arabic poetry is accessible; but I believe this book to be the first general English anthology of Asiatic verse. It is haphazard, as such books must be until some polyglot scholar gives a whole life to the matter. Variety was the only aim possible in a space so small, and therefore I have selected love poems of different centuries and of both primitive and subtle peoples."

If this—written in 1918—does not now apply in substance, it still defines my husband's attitude to these Collections.

R. C. M.

February, 1944.

INTRODUCTION

(from the *Garden of Bright Waters*`

HEAD in hand, I look at the paper leaf,
It is still white.

I look at the ink
Dry on the end of my brush.

My soul sleeps.
Will it ever wake?

I walk a little in the pouring of the sun
And pass my hands over the higher flowers.

There is the soft green forest,
There are the sweet lines of the mountains
Carved with snow, red in the sunlight.

I see the slow march of the clouds,
I hear the crows jeering, and I come back

To sit and look at the paper leaf,
Which is still white
Under my brush.

From the Chinese of Chang-Chi (770-850).

LOVE SONGS OF ASIA

SHADE OF THE ORANGE LEAVES

The young girl that in her chamber from dawn till
    eve alone
Broiders silk flowers on robes, deliciously shudders
At the unexpected sound of a far flute;
It seems to her that the voice of a young man is kissing
    her ear.

And when across the oiled paper
Of the high windows the orange leaves
Come and touch and make their shadows run on her
    knees
It seems to her that a hand is tearing her robe of silk.

From the Chinese of Tin-Tun-Ling.

THE DALLIANCE OF THE LEOPARDS

Very afraid
I saw the dalliance of the leopards.
In the beauty of their coats
They sought each other and embraced.
Had I gone between them then
And pulled them asunder by their manes,
I would have run less risk
Than when I passed in my boat
And saw you standing on a dead tree
Ready to dive and kindle the river.

From the Sanskrit (5th Century).

BLACK HAIR

Last night my kisses drowned in the softness of black
hair,
And my kisses like bees went plundering the softness
of black hair.
Last night my hands were thrust in the mystery of
black hair,
And my kisses like bees went plundering the sweetness
of pomegranates
And among the scents of the harvest above my queen's
neck, the harvest of black hair;
And my teeth played with the golden skin of her two
ears.
Last night my kisses drowned in the softness of black
hair,
And my kisses like bees went plundering the softness
of black hair.

—Your kisses went plundering the scents of my harvest,
O friend,
And the scents laid you drunk at my side. As sleep
overcame Bahram
In the bed of Sarasya, so sleep overcame you on my
bed.
I know one that has sworn your hurt for stealing the
roses from my cheeks,
Has sworn your hurt even to death, the Guardian of
black hair.
—Last night my kisses drowned in the softness of black
hair,
And my kisses like bees went plundering the softness
of black hair.

My hurt, darling? The sky will guard me if you wish
me guarded.

But now for my defence, dearest, roll me a cudgel of
black hair;

And give me the whiteness of your face, I am hungry
for it like a young bird.

Still, if you wish me there, loosen me among the
wantonness of black hair.

Last night my kisses drowned in the softness of black
hair,

And my kisses like bees went plundering the softness
of black hair.

Sweet friend, I will part the curtain of black hair and
let you into the white garden of my breast.

But I fear you will despise me and not look back when
you go away.

I am so beautiful and so white that the lamp-light
faints to see my face,

And also God has given me for adornment my heavy
black hair.

—Last night my kisses drowned in the softness of black
hair,

And my kisses like bees went plundering the softness
of black hair.

He has made you beautiful even among his most
  beautiful;
I am your little slave. O queen, cast me a little look.
I sent you the message of love at the dawn of day,
But my heart is stung by a snake, the snake of black
  hair.
Last night my kisses drowned in the softness of black
  hair,
And my kisses like bees went plundering the softness
  of black hair.

—Fear not, dear friend, I am the Charmer,
My breath will charm the snake upon your heart;
But who will charm the snake on my honour, my sad
  honour?
If you love me, let us go from Pakli. My husband is
  horrible.
From this forth I give you command over black hair.
—Last night my kisses drowned in the softness of black
  hair,
And my kisses like bees went plundering the softness
  of black hair.

Muhammadji has power over the poets of Pakli,
He takes tax from the Amirs of great Delhi.
He reigns over an empire and governs with a sceptre
  of black hair.
Last night my kisses drowned in the softness of black
  hair,
And my kisses like bees went plundering the softness
  of black hair.

From the Afghan of Muhammadji (19th Century).

THE GARDEN OF BAMBOOS

I live all alone, and I am a young girl.
I write long letters and do not know anyone to send
  them to.
Most tender things speak in my heart
And I can only say them to the bamboos in the garden.
Waiting on my feet, lifting the mat a little behind the
  door,
All day I watch the shadows of the people that pass.

A Street Song of Annam.

EYES THAT MOVE NOT

The ashes are cold in the gold of the
      perfume-brazier. It is shaped like a
      fantastic lion.

Feverishly I fidget under the red wave
      of my bed-clothes, and suddenly I throw
      them from me to get up.

But I have not the courage to undertake
      my hair-dressing, the comb is too heavy
      for my dejection.

I leave the dust to tarnish the precious
      things on my toilet-table.

Already the sun has reached the height of
      the hasp that holds up the curtain.

6

This grief that I have hidden from all,
      this grief at a departure threatening,
      becomes more bitter still.

Things to say come as far as my lips,
      and I press them back into my heart.

It is indeed a new thing for me to feel
      a torment; this is not an illness caused
      by getting drunk, nor by the melancholy
      of approaching Autumn.

      .   .   .   .

Ah, it is finished, it is finished.
He goes away to-day.

If I sang ten thousand times the
      "Stay here by me" song, yet he
      would not stay.

Now my mind has gone on a journey to the
      South; to his country, which is very far away.

Look, see, the mist encumbers my pavilion;
      before my eyes is but the water running round
      about.   It is my grief's sole witness, and may be
      astonished to reflect so long and long the
      stupefaction of my eyes that move not.

Ah, heavier still, hereafter, shall my regard
      weigh down on you, pale mirror; for even as
      I speak it is accomplished, this harm,
      this sadness of eyes that move not.

                      From the Chinese of Ly-Y-Han.

GHAZAL

If the proud girl I love would cast a glance behind her,
As down the road she swings in her bright palanquin,
She would see her lover on foot, with empty hands.

Like the white buds of tuberose in a dark night
Through the lines of betel shine out her white teeth.

When she puts henna on her hands and dives in the
soft river
One would think one saw fire twisting and running
in the water.

From the Hindustani of Dilsoz (18*th Century*).

DOUBT

Will he be true to me?
That I do not know.
But since the dawn
I have had as much disorder in my thoughts
As in my black hair.

From the Japanese of Hori-Kawa.

SONG

Like the fine and silky hair of our goats
Which climb up very high on the peaks
Of inaccessible Kara-Koroum,
So fine and silky is the hair of my girl.

Her eyes are soft as the eyes of the goats
That call their males on the mountain,
Her eyes are soft as the eyes of the goats
That hold the heavy teat to their young.

Her eyes have the colour of topaz
With which she decks her head and neck
And this topaz has the soft colour
Of the soft eyes, very soft eyes of our goats.

Her body apt for work is slight and supple,
As slight and supple as the bounds
Which our goats make, when they leap
On the curved flanks of the summit of Dapsang.

Her cheeks are ever fresh to my lips,
Fresh like the milk I draw daily
When the goats come back to the stable
From the swelling udders that sweep the ground.

Love Song of Thibet.

DISTICH

Ah, would that I could hide within my songs
And, every time you sang them, kiss your lips.

From the Persian of Oumara (10th Century).

SONG

Since you love me and I love you
The rest matters not;
I will cut grass in the fields
And you will sell it for beasts.

Since you love me and I love you
The rest matters not;
I will sow maize in the fields
And you will sell it for people.

Kafiristan.

SONG

You would climb after nectarines
In your little green jacket and puffy white drawers;
So that you fell and I caught you.
You made as if to break away,
And then settled wriggling in my arms,
All your lightness and softness were pressed against me,
And your face looked up from my breast
Puckered with amusement.
It would be something of the sort
If our clear blue night full of white stars
Turned to a night of coloured stars—
Red and purple and green to the zenith,
And orange and light violet and lemon,
And bright rose and crimson all about the sky.

From the Chinese (19*th Century*).

LOVE SONG

I

The mountains of Bech-Parma are great enough,
But my love is greater.

The glaciers that marble their tops are white,
But your breasts are whiter.

The antelope stricken by my bullet
Weeps a red blood from its wound

Which dyes with large red flowers
The field of the blowing jasmine flowers of snow.

Your arms are whiter than the jasmine flower of snow;
And your kiss is redder than the blood of the antelope.

The mountains of Bech-Parma are great enough,
But my love is greater.

II

The wind screaming in the forest when the wind of
   Russia blows
Is milder than the desire that draws me to thee.

Your body smells richer than the resin
That weeps in the sun from slender pines.

And your mouth has more of odours
Than mint flowers throw on the air.

When you are by my side, I feel in my body
A warmth more suave than the softest sun-rays.

And when you go away from me, my sadness
Is blacker than the lowering night great with storm.

The wind screaming in the forest when the wind of
    Russia blows
Is milder than the desire that draws me to thee.

Daghestan.

SONG

Dew on the bamboos,
Cooler than dew on the bamboos
Is putting my cheek against your breasts.

The pit of green and black snakes,
I would rather be in the pit of green and black snakes
Than be in love with you.

From the Sanskrit (5th Century).

GHAZAL

Seeing me come the heavenly girl fled very fast,
And ran surpassing fast, her tongue between her teeth.
I followed, and the heavenly girl at the noise of my
    following
Pulled back the leaf of the door and hid behind.
I followed, and for her savagery fast, fast I scolded her;
Till all ashamed and drawing back she could not
    answer me. . . .
Why starts the morning cock his chant so fast, so fast?
An evil cock, an evil chant to shatter my delight . . .
And this song is only as threads of smoke to the
    heavenly girl,
That vanish surpassing fast upon the winds of Spring.

From the Hindustani of Inscha (18th Century).

SPRING COLD

In the melancholy enclosure

The wind leans, and drags at the threads of fine rain.

It is a good thing the double doors are shut.

The grace of the willows, the frailness of the
    flowers, these bow down before the capricious
    weather that rains towards the time of "Cold
    Feasts."

But whatever the weather, it is always difficult
    to find the balanced harmony of verse.

In the meanwhile: this much poetry is finished.

      ·   ·   ·   ·

What sweet thing may sustain, what sweet thing
    may console him who wakes from drunkenness? . . .
    the drunkenness of poetry, which is other than
    the drunkenness of wine? . . .

The wild swans have just passed.

Ah, I have a thousand sad things which I would
    confide to these rapid riders.

      ·   ·   ·   ·

In these days the Spring cold can be felt
    in the upper storey.

On four sides the blinds are down in front
    of the windows.

I am too dissatisfied to go and lean on
    the jade balustrade.

The coverlet is cold. All the perfume is burned away.

I wake from my last dream.

Why are not people with great sorrows
    forbidden to dream?

The colourless dew is falling into the water.

The trees are getting green again.

Quite a lot of people will rejoice to see
    the Spring come back.

The sun is coming out, the mist is drifting away.

To-day I suppose I will have to look at some more
    fine weather.

                  From the Chinese of Ly-Y-Han.

SONG

If you love God, take your mirror between your hands
    and look
How beautiful are your breasts with their two russet
    berries.
At sight of them, stricken, drunken, I cannot make a
    distinction
Between them and white roses beaten in white snow.
How beautiful are your breasts with their two russet
    berries.

14

No soul could be strong against your so bright eyes,
My desire hungers, for the kisses of one night did not
    fill it.
For love of God, take your mirror between your hands
    and judge
If a man could tire in looking on your face.
My desire hungers, for the kisses of one night did not
    fill it;
How beautiful are your breasts with their two russet
    berries.

From the Turkish of Mahmud Djellaladin Pasha
(19th Century).

MOKCHA
(Supreme Happiness)

Like the bright drop
Which, from the perfumed womanhood
Of loving night,
Night amorous ever,
Tireless in her couplings
With the body of the world,
Falls in the virgin breast
Of a rose, and straightway
Ravishes her and shows
In its tiny globe
All the work of Brahma,
All the sky and all the earth;

So the drop of the dew
Of thy love, which trembles
On the petals of my heart,
Reflects in my love
The sky of the soul,
So sought Nirvana;
My love is Mokcha
Making me, from on earth,
Taste the high savour
Of immaterial joy.
Through thy love I have felt
That my essence is god-like
And that I am part
Of the world's Creator.

From the Burmese of Megdan (19*th Century*).

GHAZAL

When you have thrown torture and desire, O cruel
  child,
Into your lover's heart with lissom coquetries,
You sit down, calm and unmoved and never noticing,
And put desirous order into the loosened tangles of
  your hair.

And I watching you think of a placid pilgrim
That has come to camp and sits taking his ease,
With never a thought for his fellows on the road.
And I watching you think of the unconscious earth
Carelessly drinking the tears from wounded hearts.

From the Hindustani of Isch (18*th Century*).

VAI! TCHODJOUKLAREUM!

Ah! my children! do you know Djemileh,
The turquoise, the carnation, the most beautiful girl
   in Bagdad?
Ah! my children!

Ah! my children! her face has aspects of the moon,
And in each of her eyes there is a sun.
Ah! my children!

Ah! my children! sometimes she leaves her vest un-
   fastened,
Forgetting—who knows?—that it hides her breasts.
Ah! my children!

Ah! my children! she has round rosy paps
Standing straight out like peaches not yet ripe.
Ah! my children!

Ah! my children! look at the curve of her back;
She might crack nuts below her waist there.
Ah! my children!

Ah! my children! what shall be said of her thighs,
What so good to dream of as her thighs?
Ah! my children!

Ah! my children! Djemileh has just passed
Appetising and gilt like a cake for Ramazan.
Ah! my children!

Ah! my children! she comes down from the mountains
With her arms full of flowers, those little flowers that
    never die.
Ah! my children!

Ah! my children! the wind makes cling to her skin
Her rose robe, and makes her look quite naked.
Ah! my children!

Ah! my children! Djemileh comes to us to sell
The little flowers that never die, plucked in the moun-
    tain.
Ah! my children!

Ah! my children! when she sells her flowers
The bright eyes of the lads bathe her and devour her.
Ah! my children!

Ah! my children! eyes that pass through her robe
And do not count the money she gives back.
Ah! my children!

Ah! my children! feeling hands that tickle her
And she laughs with all her teeth, pulling back her
    veil.
Ah! my children!

Ah! my children! Djemileh has sold the flowers from
    the mountain;
And added to her dowry for marrying the hill boy she
    loves.
Ah! my children!

                                        Kurdistan.

18

SUBMISSION

When you have bathed in the river
On the moon's third day,
You make yourself, ah, so the more to be desired
By slipping on a robe the colour of your body.
Tell me, child, are three baskets of saffron enough
To colour your breasts and your arms and your face?

No other girl knows, like you, how to entice me,
Walking alone in the shadows of the palm trees.
None has your tickling gestures, your enflaming eyes—
So young, so smooth, and so flower fresh,
You must have more men silly about you
Than there are corners in your bedroom to hide them.

In the morning when I come to see you under the
    verandah
Just for the pleasure of talking to you;
Or in the evening when I curry favour with the
    poulterer
Just for the pleasure of feeling myself near you;
Or at night when my hand seeks to clasp you
Through the hole pierced in the planking by your bed;
Your mother can say all she likes,
Reproaches, insults, swear-words.   I accept all in
    advance.
But I conjure you do not refuse me
A quite small corner of your bedroom in which to hide.

From the Siamese.

IN THE PALACE

What rigorous calm! What almost holy silence!
All the doors are shut, and the beds of flowers
    are giving out scent; discreetly, of course. . . .

Two women that lean against each other, stand to
    the balustrade of red marble on the edge of the
    terrace.

One of them wishes to speak, to confide to her
    friend the secret sorrow that is agonizing her heart.

She throws an anxious glance at the motionless leaves,
    and because of a paroquet with iridescent wings
    that perches on a branch, she sighs and is silent.

From the Chinese of Tu-Sin-Yu.

A THING REMEMBERED

I'll not forget the warm blue night when my bold girl,
Whose kissing lips smell sweet of honey and of rose
    water,

Came softly to my room, and my room glowed
As if the moon at her bright full had entered to me.

"Press me in your arms," she said. "All that your love
    demands
Ask and obtain. My old watching woman is far away."

I pressed her in my arms, and said: "Your robe is a curtain.
Wherefore a curtain between me and thee, violet joy of my heart?"

And so saying, I began to undo some parts of her robe.
She looked smiling at me and I, also smiling, unloosed and unloosed.

"My joy, the flower in her bud pleases me not:
And fruit hanging under leaves delights me not.

"My sword I love not in its sheath, it is no pleasure
To see the stars of night hidden behind clouds."

From the Arabic.

THE MOST VIRTUOUS WOMAN

Pluck the most beautiful apricot from this tree
And place it on silk in a coffer of sandal-wood;
At the end of three days the silk
Will be stained by the juice of the fruit.

Choose the most virtuous woman from this world,
Place her image in the coffer of your heart,
Even on the same instant your heart
Will be soiled with bad thoughts.

Popular Song of Manchuria.

THE MEETING

A summer's night I met my girl on the path
That leads straight to her dwelling and straight to my
    tent.

We were alone, we two, without watchers or informers,
Far from the tribe, far from jealous eyes and spying
        ears and harming tongues.

I laid my face on the ground, my brow a footstool for
    my girl.
She said: "Open your heart with joy, we are without
    watchers;
Come press your lips to my veil."

But my lips would not consent to it.
I felt that I had two honours to guard,
My girl's and mine.

And, as was my desire, we were all night together,
Near to each other, far from the tribe and spying eyes.

And it seemed that I was master
Of all the kingdoms of the world, and that the elements
Obeyed me as slaves.

From the Arabic of Ibn-el-Farad (A.D. 1220).

THE TRYST

In thy presence my arms, my hands, my lips, all my
    being,
Tremble as tremble the leaves
Of the cinnamon-apples shaken by the wind.

—The leaves of the cinnamon-apple do not tremble, O
    my love.
They shiver under the caress of the wind
Which drinks deep of their perfumed kisses.

Come with me to-night under the cinnamon-apples
And like their leaves you will shiver under my caress,
And like the wind I will drink deep of your perfumed
    kisses.

I will come. But what will you give me for my kisses?
—For your kisses I offer you my kisses.
What will you give me for my heart?
—For your heart I offer you my heart.
What will you give me for my love?
—For your love I offer you my life.

I accept your kisses and your heart and your life;
And I give in exchange myself to be all yours.
And all trembling this night I will come to offer you
    my kisses
Under the cinnamon-apples caressed by the wind
And in the wind that drinks deep of their perfumed
    kisses.

By an unknown author of Cambodia.

RUBAIYAT

They've assured me that Paradise is full of girls,
They've assured me that I'll find wine and honey in
    Paradise.
Well then, why forbid me wine and girls down here,
Seeing that up there my reward will be girls and wine?

From the Persian of Omar Khayyám (10th Century).

PICTURE

I see the snowy winter sky through the old arch;
And in the middle the line of one tree.
A flight of crows comes just above the tree,
Sweeping to left and right, and tailing out behind.
I think of you.

From the Japanese (18th Century).

WHITE

I thought that it was snowing
Flowers. But, no. It was this young lady
Coming towards me.

*From the Japanese of Yori-Kito
(19th Century).*

BLACK MARIGOLDS

"And sometimes we look to the end of the tale that there should be marriage-feasts, and find only, as it were, black marigolds and a silence."

AZEDDIN EL MOCADECCI.

BLACK MARIGOLDS

Even now
My thought is all of this gold-tinted king's daughter
With garlands tissue and golden buds,
Smoke tangles of her hair, and sleeping or waking
Feet trembling in love, full of pale languor;
My thought is clinging as to a lost learning
Slipped down out of the minds of men,
Labouring to bring her back into my soul.

Even now
If I see in my soul the citron-breasted fair one
Still gold-tinted, her face like our night stars,
Drawing unto her; her body beaten about with flame,
Wounded by the flaring spear of love,
My first of all by reason of her fresh years,
Then is my heart buried alive in snow.

Even now
If my girl with lotus eyes came to me again
Weary with the dear weight of young love,
Again I would give her to these starved twins of arms
And from her mouth drink down the heavy wine,
As a reeling pirate bee in fluttered ease
Steals up the honey from the nenuphar.

Even now
I bring her back, ah, wearied out with love
So that her slim feet could not bear her up;
Curved falls of her hair down on her white cheeks;
In the confusion of her coloured vests
Speaking that guarded giving up, and her scented arms
Lay like cool bindweed over against my neck.

Even now
I bring her back to me in her quick shame,
Hiding her bright face at the point of day:
Making her grave eyes move in watered stars,
For love's great sleeplessness wandering all night,
Seeming to sail gently, as that pink bird,
Down the water of love in a harvest of lotus.

Even now
If I saw her lying all wide eyes
And with collyrium the indent of her cheek
Lengthened to the bright ear and her pale side
So suffering the fever of my distance,
Then would my love for her be ropes of flowers, and
    night
A black-haired lover on the breasts of day.

Even now
I see the heavy startled hair of this reed-flute player
Who curved her poppy lips to love dances,
Having a youth's face madding like the moon
Lying at her full; limbs ever moving a little in love,
Too slight, too delicate, tired with the small burden
Of bearing love ever on white feet.

Even now
She is present to me on her beds,
Balmed with the exhalation of a flattering musk,
Rich with the curdy essence of santal;
Girl with eyes dazing as the seeded wine,
Showing as a pair of gentle nut-hatches
Kissing each other with their bills, each hidden
By turns within a little grasping mouth.

27

Even now
She swims back in the crowning hour of love
All red with wine her lips have given to drink,
Soft round the mouth with camphor and faint blue
Tinted upon the lips, her slight body,
Her great live eyes, the colourings of herself
A clear perfection; sighs of musk outstealing
And powdered wood spice heavy of Kashmir.

Even now
I see her; far face blond like gold
Rich with small lights, and tinted shadows surprised
Over and over all of her; with glittering eyes
All bright for love but very love weary,
As it were the conjuring disk of the moon when Rahu
    ceases
With his dark stumbling block to hide her rays.

Even now
She is art-magically present to my soul,
And that one word of strange heart's ease, goodbye,
That in the night, in loth moving to go,
And bending over to a golden mouth,
I said softly to the turned away
Tenderly tired hair of this king's daughter.

Even now
My eyes that hurry to see no more are painting,
    painting
Faces of my lost girl. O golden rings
That tap against cheeks of small magnolia leaves,
O whitest so soft parchment where
My poor divorcèd lips have written excellent
Stanzas of kisses, and will write no more.

Even now
Death sends me the flickering of powdery lids
Over wild eyes and the pity of her slim body
All broken up with the weariness of joy;
The little red flowers of her breasts to be my comfort
Moving above scarves, and for my sorrow
Wet crimson lips that once I marked as mine.

Even now
By a cool noise of waters in the spring
The Asoka with young flowers that feign her fingers
And bud in red; and in the green vest pearls kissing
As it were rose leaves in the gardens of God; the
  shining at night
Of white cheeks in the dark; smiles from light thoughts
  within,
And her walking as of a swan: these trouble me.

Even now
The pleasèd intimacy of rough love
Upon the patient glory of her form
Racks me with memory; and her bright dress
As it were yellow flame, which the white hand
Shamefastly gathers in her rising haste,
The slender grace of her departing feet.

Even now
When all my heavy heart is broken up
I seem to see my prison walls breaking
And then a light, and in that light a girl
Her fingers busied about her hair, her cool white arms
Faint rosy at the elbows, raised in the sunlight,
And temperate eyes that wander far away.

Even now
I seem to see my prison walls come close,
Built up of darkness, and against that darkness
A girl no taller than my breast and very tired,
Leaning upon the bed and smiling, feeding
A little bird and lying slender as ash trees,
Sleepily aware as I told of the green
Grapes and the small bright coloured river flowers.

Even now
I see her, as I used, in her white palace
Under black torches throwing cool red light,
Woven with many flowers and tearing the dark.
I see her rising, showing all her face
Defiant timidly, saying clearly:
Now I shall go to sleep, good-night, my ladies.

Even now
Though I am so far separate, a flight of birds
Swinging from side to side over the valley trees,
Passing my prison with their calling and crying,
Bring me to see my girl. For very bird-like
Is her song singing, and the state of a swan
In her light walking, like the shaken wings
Of a black eagle falls her nightly hair.

Even now
I know my princess was happy. I see her stand
Touching her breasts with all her flower-soft fingers,
Looking askance at me with smiling eyes.
There is a god that arms him with a flower
And she was stricken deep. Here, oh die here.
Kiss me and I shall be purer than quick rivers.

Even now
They chatter her weakness through the two bazaars
Who was so strong to love me. And small men
That buy and sell for silver being slaves
Crinkle the fat about their eyes; and yet
No Prince of the Cities of the Sea has taken her,
Leading to his grim bed. Little lonely one,
You clung to me as a garment clings; my girl.

Even now
Only one dawn shall rise for me. The stars
Revolve to-morrow's night and I not heed.
One brief cold watch beside an empty heart
And that is all. This night she rests not well;
Oh, sleep; for there is heaviness for all the world
Except for the death-lighted heart of me.

Even now
My sole concern the slipping of her vests,
Her little breasts the life beyond this life.
One night of disarray in her green hems,
Her golden cloths, outweighs the order of earth,
Making of none effect the tides of the sea.
I have seen her enter the temple meekly and there seem
The flag of flowers that veils the very god.

Even now
I mind the coming and talking of wise men from towers
Where they had thought away their youth. And I,
    listening,
Found not the salt of the whispers of my girl,
Murmur of confused colours, as we lay near sleep;
Little wise words and little witty words,
Wanton as water, honied with eagerness.

31

Even now
I call to mind her weariness in the morning
Close lying in my arms, and tiredly smiling
At my disjointed prayer for her small sake.
Now in my morning the weariness of death
Sends me to sleep. Had I made coffins
I might have lived singing to three score.

Even now
The woodcutter and the fisherman turn home,
With on his axe the moon and in his dripping net
Caught yellow moonlight. The purple flame of fires
Calls them to love and sleep. From the hot town
The maker of scant songs for bread wanders
To lie under the clematis with his girl.
The moon shines on her breasts, and I must die.

Even now
I have a need to make up prayers, to speak
My last consideration of the world
To the great thirteen gods, to make my balance
Ere the soul journeys on. I kneel and say:
Father of Light. Leave we it burning still
That I may look at you. *Mother of the Stars,*
Give me your feet to kiss; I love you, dear.

Even now
I seem to see the face of my lost girl
With frightened eyes, like a wood wanderer,
In travail with sorrowful waters, unwept tears
Labouring to be born and fall; when white face turned
And little ears caught at the far murmur,
The pleased snarling of the tumult of dogs
When I was hurried away down the white road.

Even now
When slow rose-yellow moons looked out at night
To guard the sheaves of harvest and mark down
The peach's fall, how calm she was and love worthy.
Glass-coloured starlight falling as thin as dew
Was wont to find us at the spirit's starving time
Slow straying in the orchard paths with love.

Even now
Love is a god and Rati the dark his bride;
But once I found their child and she was fairer,
That could so shine. And we were each to each
Wonderful and a presence not yet felt
In any dream. I knew the sunset earth
But as a red gold ring to bear my emerald
Within the little summer of my youth.

Even now
I marvel at the bravery of love.
She, whose two feet might be held in one hand
And all her body on a shield of the guards,
Lashed like a gold panther taken in a pit
Tearfully valiant, when I too was taken;
Bearding her black beard father in his wrath,
Striking the soldiers with white impotent hands.

Even now
I mind that I loved cypress and roses, dear,
The great blue mountains and the small grey hills,
The sounding of the sea. Upon a day
I saw strange eyes and hands like butterflies;
For me at morning larks flew from the thyme
And children came to bathe in little streams.

Even now
Sleep left me all these nights for your white bed
And I am sure you sistered lay with sleep
After much weeping. Piteous little love,
Death is in the garden, time runs down,
The year that simple and unexalted ran till now
Ferments in winy autumn, and I must die.

Even now
I mind our going, full of bewilderment
As who should walk from sleep into great light,
Along the running of the winter river,
A dying sun on the cool hurrying tide
No more by green rushes delayed in dalliance,
With a clear purpose in his flower flecked length
Informed, to reach Nirvana and the sea.

Even now
I love long black eyes that caress like silk,
Ever and ever sad and laughing eyes,
Whose lids make such sweet shadow when they close
It seems another beautiful look of hers.
I love a fresh mouth, ah, a scented mouth,
And curving hair, subtle as a smoke,
And light fingers, and laughter of green gems.

Even now
I mind asking: Where love and how love Rati's
    priestesses?
You can tell me of their washings at moon down
And if that warm basin have silver borders.
Is it so that when they comb their hair
Their fingers, being purple stained, show
Like coral branches in the black sea of their hair?

Even now
I remember that you made answer very softly,
We being one soul, your hand on my hair,
The burning memory rounding your near lips:
I have seen the priestesses of Rati make love at moon
  fall
And then in a carpeted hall with a bright gold lamp
Lie down carelessly anywhere to sleep.

Even now
I have no surety that she is not Mahadevi
Rose red of Siva, or Kapagata
The wilful ripe Companion of the King,
Or Krishna's own Lakshmi, the violet haired.
I am not certain but that dark Brahma
In his high secret purposes
Has sent my soft girl down to make the three worlds
  mad
With capering about her scented feet.

Even now
Call not the master painters from all the world,
Their thin black boards, their rose and green and grey,
Their ashes of lapis lazuli ultramarine,
Their earth of shadows the umber. Laughing at art
Sunlight upon the body of my bride,
For painting not nor any eyes for ever.
Oh warm tears on the body of my bride.

Even now
I mind when the red crowds were passed and it was
    raining
How glad those two that shared the rain with me;
For they talked happily with rich young voices
And at the storm's increase, closer and with content,
Each to the body of the other held
As there were no more severance for ever.

Even now
The stainless fair appearance of the moon
Rolls her gold beauty over an autumn sky
And the stiff anchorite forgets to pray;
How much the sooner I, if her wild mouth
Tasting of the taste of manna came to mine
And kept my soul at balance above a kiss.

Even now
Her mouth carelessly scented as with lotus dust
Is water of love to the great heat of love,
A tirtha very holy, a lover's lake
Utterly sacred. Might I go down to it
But one time more, then should I find a way
To hold my lake for ever and ever more
Sobbing out my life beside the waters.

Even now
I mind that the time of the falling of blossoms started
    my dream
Into a wild life, into my girl;
Then was the essence of her beauty spilled
Down on my days so that it fades not,
Fails not, subtle and fresh, in perfuming
That day, and the days, and this the latest day.

Even now
She with young limbs as smooth as flower pollen,
Whose swaying body is laved in the cool
Waters of languor, this dear bright-coloured bird,
Walks not, changes not, advances not
Her weary station by the black lake
Of Gone Forever, in whose fountain vase
Balance the water-lilies of my thought.

Even now
Spread we our nets beyond the farthest rims
So surely that they take the feet of dawn
Before you wake and after you are sleeping
Catch up the visible and invisible stars
And web the ports the strongest dreamer dreamed,
Yet is it all one, Vidya, yet is it nothing.

Even now
The night is full of silver straws of rain,
And I will send my soul to see your body
This last poor time. I stand beside your bed;
Your shadowed head lies leaving a bright space
Upon the pillow empty, your sorrowful arm
Holds from your side and clasps not anything.
There is no covering upon you.

Even now
I think your feet seek mine to comfort them.
There is some dream about you even now
Which I'll not hear at waking. Weep not at dawn,
Though day brings wearily your daily loss
And all the light is hateful. Now is it time
To bring my soul away.

Even now
I mind that I went round with men and women,
And underneath their brows, deep in their eyes,
I saw their souls, which go slipping aside
In swarms before the pleasure of my mind;
The world was like a flight of birds, shadow or flame
Which I saw pass above the engraven hills.
Yet was there never one like to my girl.

Even now
Death I take up as consolation.
Nay, were I free as the condor with his wings
Or old kings throned on violet ivory,
Night would not come without beds of green floss
And never a bed without my bright darling.
It is most fit that you strike now, black guards,
And let this fountain out before the dawn.

Even now
I know that I have savoured the hot taste of life
Lifting green cups and gold at the great feast.
Just for a small and a forgotten time
I have had full in my eyes from off my girl
The whitest pouring of eternal light.
The heavy knife. As to a gala day.

From the Sanskrit of Chauras
(*Chaura-panchasika*, 1st *Century*).

THE GARDEN OF BRIGHT WATERS

BALLADE OF NUR UDDIN

I have seen a small proud face brimming with sunlight;
I have seen the daughter of the King of Qulzum
    passing from grace to grace.
Yesterday she threw her bed on the floor of her double
    house
And laughed with a thousand graces.
She has a little pearl and coral cap
And rides in a palanquin with servants about her
And claps her hands, being too proud to call.
I have seen a small proud face brimming with sun-
    light.

"My palanquin is truly green and blue;
I fill the world with pomp and take my pleasure;
I make men run up and down before me,
And am not as young a girl as you pretend.
I am of Iran, of a powerful house, I am pure steel.
I hear that I am spoken of in Lahore."
I have seen a small proud face brimming with sun-
    light.

I also hear that they speak of you in Lahore,
You walk with a joyous step,
Your nails are red and the palms of your hands are
    rosy.
A pear-tree with a fresh stem is in your palace gardens,
I would not that your mother should give my pear-
    tree
To twine with an evil spice-tree or fool banana.
I have seen a small proud face brimming with sun-
    light.

"The coins that my father gave me for my forehead
Throw rays and light the hearts of far men;
The ray of light from my red ring is sharper than a
    diamond.
I go about and about in pride as of hemp wine
And my words are chosen.
But I give you my honey cheeks, dear, I trust them to
    you."
I have seen a small proud face brimming with sun-
    light.

The words of my mouth are coloured and shining
    things;
And two great saints are my perpetual guards.
There is never a song of *Nur Uddin* but has in it a great
    achievement
And is as brilliant as a young hyacinth;
I pour a ray of honey on my disciples,
There is as it were a fire in my ballades.
I have seen a small proud face brimming with sun-
    light.

From the Pus'hto (Afghans, 19th Century).

COME, MY BELOVED!

Come, my beloved! And I say again: Come, my
    beloved!
The doves are moaning and calling and will not cease.
    Come, my beloved!

"The fairies have made me queen, and my heart is
    love.
Sweeter than the green cane is my red mouth."
        Come, my beloved!

The jacinth has spilled odour on your hair,
The balance of your neck is like a jacinth;
You have set a star of green between your brows.
        Come, my beloved!

Like lemon-trees among the rocks of grey hills
Are the soft colours of the airy veil
To your rose knee from your curved almond waist.
        Come, my beloved!

Your light breast veil is tawny brown with stags,
Stags with eyes of emerald, hunted by red kings.
        Come, my beloved!

Muhammad Din is wandering; he is drunken and mad;
For a year he has been dying. Send for the doctor!
        Come, my beloved!

From the Pus'hto of Muhammad Din Tilai
(Afghans, 19th Century).

GHAZAL OF TAVAKKUL

To-day I saw Laila's breasts, the hills of a fair city
From which my heart might leap to heaven.

Her breasts are a garden of white roses
Having two drifted hills of fallen rose-leaves.

Her breasts are a garden where doves are singing
And doves are moaning with arrows because of her.

All her body is a flower and her face is Shalibagh;
She has fruits of beautiful colours and the doves abide
there.

Over the garden of her breasts she combs the gold rain
of her hair. . . .
You have killed *Tavakkul*, the faithful pupil of Abdel
Qadir Gilani.

From the Pus'hto (Afghans, 19th Century).

GHAZAL OF SAYYID AHMAD

My heart is torn by the tyranny of women very quietly;
Day and night my tears are wearing away my cheeks
very quietly.

Life is a red thing like the sun setting very quietly;
Setting quickly and heavily and very quietly.

If you are to buy heaven by a good deed, to-day the
market is open;
To-morrow is a day when no man buys,
And the caravan is broken up very quietly.

The kings are laughing and the slaves are laughing;
but for your sake
Sayyid Ahmad is walking and mourning very quietly.

From the Pus'hto (Afghans, 19th Century)

GHAZAL, IN LAMENT FOR THE DEAD, OF PIR MUHAMMAD

The season of parting has come up with the wind;
My girl has hollowed my heart with the hot iron of
  separation.

Keep away, doctor, your roots and your knives are
  useless.
None ever cured the ills of the ill of separation.

There is no one near me noble enough to be told;
I tear my collar in the "Alas! Alas!" of separation.

She was a branch of santal; she closed her eyes and
  left me.
Autumn has come and she has gone, broken to pieces
  in the wind of separation.

I am *Pir Muhammad* and I am stumbling away to die;
She stamped on my eyes with the foot of separation.
          From the Pus'hto (Afghans, 19th Century).

BALLADE OF NURSHALI

Come in haste this dusk, dear child. I will be on the
  water path
When your girl friends go laughing by the road.
"Come in haste this dusk; I have become your
  nightingale,
And the young girls leave me alone because of you.
I give you the poppy of my mouth and my fallen hair."
  Come in haste this dusk, dear child.

"I have dishevelled and spread out my hair for you;
Take my wrist, for there is no shame
And my father has gone out.
Sit near me on this red bed quietly."
    Come in haste this dusk, dear child.

"Sit near me on this red bed, I lift the poppy to your
    lips;
Your hand is strong upon my breast;
My beauty is a garden and you the bird in the flower-
    ing tree."
    Come in haste this dusk, dear child.

"My beauty is a garden with crimson flowers."
But I cannot reach over the thicket of your hair.
This is *Nurshali* sighing for the garden;
    Come in haste this dusk, dear child.

From the Pus'hto (Afghans).

GHAZAL OF MUHAMMAD DIN TILAI

The world is fainting,
And you will weep at last.

The world is fainting
And falling into a swoon.

The world is turning and changing;
The world is fainting,
And you will weep at last.

Look at the love of Farhad, who pierced a mountain
And pierced a brass hill for the love of Shirin.
The world is fainting,
And you will weep at last.

Qutab Khan of the Ranizais was in love
And death became the hostess of his lady.
The world is fainting,
And you will weep at last.

Adam loved Durkho, and they were separated.
You know the story;
There is no lasting love.
The world is fainting,
And you will weep at last.

Muhammad Din is ill for the matter of a little honey;
This is a moment to be generous.
The world is fainting,
And you will weep at last.

From the Pus'hto (*Afghans*, 19*th Century*).

MICRA

When you lie with me and love me,
You give me a second life of young gold;
And when you lie with me and love me not,
I am as one who puts out hands in the dark
And touches cold wet death.

From the Pus'hto of Mirza Rahchan Kayil
(*Afghans*, 19*th Century*).

46

GHAZAL OF MIRA

The lover to his lass: I have fallen before your door.
I came to ask for alms and have lost my all,
I had a copper-shod quarter-staff but the dogs
    attacked me,
And not a strand of her hair came the way of my lips.
The lover to his lass: I have fallen before your door.

The lamp burns and I must play the green moth.
I have stolen her scented rope of flowers,
But the women caught me and built a little gaol
About my heart with your old playthings.
The lover to his lass: I have fallen before your door.

Mira is a mountain goat that climbs to die
Upon the top peak in the rocks of grief;
It is the hour; make haste.
The lover to his lass: I have fallen before your door.
              From the Pus'hto (Afghans, 19th Century).

GHAZAL OF MIRA

The world passes, nothing lasts, and the creation of men
Is buried alive under the vault of Time.

Autumn comes pillaging gardens;
The bulbuls laugh to see the flowers falling.

Wars start up wherever your eye glances,
And the young men moan marching on to the
    batteries.

47

Mira is the unkempt old man you see on the road;
He has taken his death-wound in battle.

From the Pus'hto (Afghans, 19th Century).

GHAZAL OF ISA AKHUN ZADA

Beauty with the flame shawl, do not repulse me;
Breathing idol of rose ivory, look at me;
Beauty with the flame shawl, let me say a little thing,
Lend your small ears to my quick sighing.
Breathing idol, I have come to the walls of death;
And there are coloured cures behind the crystal of
  your eyes.
Life is a tale ill constructed without love.
Beauty of the flame shawl, do not repulse me;
I am at your door wasted and white and dying.
Breathing idol of rose ivory, look at me;
Beauty with the flame shawl, do not repulse me.

This is the salaam that slaves make, and after the
  salaam
Listen to these quick sighings and their wisdom.
All the world has spied on us and seen our love,
And in four days or five days will be whispering evil.
Knot your robes in a turban, escape and be mine for
  ever;
Beauty with the flame shawl, do not repulse me.
After that we will both of us go to prison.
Breathing idol of rose ivory, look at me;
Beauty with the flame shawl, do not repulse me.

My quick sighings carry a tender promise;
I will have time to remember in the battle,
Though all the world is a thousand whistling swords
    against me.
The iron is still in the rock that shall forge my death-
    sword,
Though I have foes more than the stars
Of a thousand valley starlights.
Breathing idol of rose ivory, look at me;
Beauty with the flame shawl, do not repulse me.

I am as strong as Sikander, I am as strong as death;
You will hear me come with guns brooding behind
    me,
And laughing bloody battalions following after.
Isa Gal is stronger than God;
Do not whip me, do not whip me,
Beauty with the flame shawl, do not repulse me;
Breathing idol of rose ivory, look at me.
Breathing idol of rose ivory, look at me;
Beauty with the flame shawl, do not repulse me.

From the Pus'hto (Afghans, 19th Century).

THE BAMBOO GARDEN

Old bamboos are about my house,
And the floor of my house is untidy with old books.
It is sweet to rest in the shade of it
And read the poems of the masters.

But I remember a delightful fisherman
Who played on the five-stringed dan in the evening.
In the day he allowed his reed canoe to float
Over the lakes and rivers,
Watching his nets and singing.

A sweet boy promised to marry me,
But he went away and left me
Like a reed canoe that rolls adrift
In the middle of a river.

Song of Annam.

STRANGER THINGS HAVE HAPPENED

Do not believe that ink is always black,
  Or lime white, or lemon sour;
You cannot ring one bell from two pagodas,
You cannot have two governors for the city of Lang
  Son.

I found you binding an orange spray
  Of flowers with white flowers;
I never noticed the flower gathering
  Of other village ladies.
Would you like me to go and see your father and
  mother?

Song of Annam.

NOCTURNE

It is late at night
And the North Star is shining.
The mist covers the rice-fields
And the bamboos
Are whispering full of crickets.
The watch beats on the iron-wood gong,
And priests are ringing the pagoda bells.
We hear the far-away games of peasants
And distant singing in the cottages.

It is late at night.
As we talk gently,
Sitting by one another,
Life is as beautiful as night.
The red moon is rising
On the mountain side
Like a fire started among the trees.

There is the North Star
Shining like a paper lantern.
The light air brings dew to our faces
And the sound of tamtams beaten far away.
Let us sit like this all night.

Song of Annam.

THE GAO FLOWER

I am the Gao flower high in a tree,
You are the grass Long Mai on the path-side.
When heat comes down after the dews of morning
The flower grows pale and tumbles on the grass,
The grass Long Mai that keeps the fallen Gao.

Folk who let their daughters grow
Without achieving a husband
Might easily forget to fence their garden,
Or let their radishes grow flower and rank
When they could eat them ripe and tender.

Come to me, you that I see walk
Every night in a red turban;
Young man with the white turban, come to me.
We will plant marrows together in a garden,
And there may be little marrows for your children.

I will dye your turban blue and red and yellow,
You with the white turban.
You that are passing with a load of water,
I call you
And you do not even turn your head.

Song of Annam.

THE GIRL OF KE-MO

I'm a girl of Ke-Mo village
Selling my rice wine on the road.
Mine is the strongest rice wine in the land,
Though my bottle is so patched and dirty.
These silly rags are not my body,
The parts you cannot see are counted pleasant;
But you are just too drunk to drink my wine,
And just too plain to lie down on my mat.
He who would drink the wine of the girl of Ke-Mo
Needs a beautiful body and a lofty wit.

Song of Annam.

GIRL OF CLEAR RIVER

Clear River twists nine times about
Clear River; but so deep
That none can see the green sand.
You hear the birds about Clear River:
Dik, dik, dik, dik, diu dik.

A girl with jade eyes
Leans on the wall of a pavilion.
She has the moonrise in her heart
And the singing of love songs
Comes to her up the river.

She stands and dreams for me
Outside the house by the bamboo door.
In a minute
I will leave my shadow
And talk to her of poetry and love.

Song of Annam.

WAITING TO MARRY A STUDENT

I still walk slowly on the river bank
Where I came singing,
And where I saw your boat pass up beyond the sun
Setting red in the river.
I want Autumn,
I want the leaves to begin falling at once,
So that the cold time may bring us close again
Like K'ien Niü and Chik Nü, the two stars.

Each year when Autumn comes
The crows make a black bridge across the milky sea,
And then these two poor stars
Can run together in gold and be at peace.
Darling, for my sake work hard
And be received with honour at the Examinations.

Since I saw your boat pass up beyond the sun
I have forgotten how to sing
And how to paddle the canoe across the lake.
I know how to sit down and how to be sad,
And I know how to say nothing;
But every other art has slipped away.

Song of Annam.

A SONG FOR TWO

I have lacquered my teeth to find a husband.

And I have need of a wife.
Give me a kiss and they will marry us
At Mo-Lao, my village.

I will marry you if you will wait for me.
Wait till the banana puts forth branches,
And fruit hangs heavy on the Sung-tree,
And the onion flowers;
Wait till the dove goes down in the pool to lay her eggs,
And the eel climbs into a tree to make her nest.

Song of Annam.

LOVE BROWN AND BITTER

You know so well how to stay me with vapours
Distilled expertly to that unworthy end;
You know the poses of your body I love best
And that I am cheerful with your head on my breast;
You know you please me by disliking one friend;
You read up what amuses me in the papers.

Who knows me knows I am not of those fools
That gets tired of a woman who is kind to them,
Yet you know not how stifled you render me
By learning me so well, how I long to see
An unpractised girl under your clever phlegm,
A soul not so letter-perfect in the rules.

From the Arabic of John Duncan.

LYING DOWN ALONE

I shall never see your tired sleep
In the bed that you make beautiful,
Nor hardly ever be a dream
That plays by your dark hair;
Yet I think I know your turning sigh
And your trusting arm's abandonment,
For they are the picture of my night,
My night that does not end.

From the Arabic of John Duncan.

WHITE AND GREEN AND BLACK TEARS

Why are your tears so white?
Dear, I have wept so long
That my old tears grow white like my old hair.

Why are your tears so green?
Dear, the waters are wept away
And the green gall is flowing.

Why are your tears so black?
Dear, the weeping is over
And the black flash you loved is breaking.

From the Arabic (School of Ebn-el-Farid)
(13th Century).

A CONCEIT

I hide my love,
I will not say her name.
And yet since I confess
I love, her name is told.
You know that if I love
It must be . . . Whom?

From the Arabic of Ebn Kalakis Abu El
Fath Nasrallsh (11th Century).

VALUES

Since there is excitement
In suffering for a woman,
Let him burn on.
The dust in a wolf's eyes
Is balm of flowers to the wolf
When a flock of sheep has raised it.

From the Arabic.

THE GREAT OFFENCE

She seemed so bored,
I wanted to embrace her by surprise;
But then the scalding waters
Fell from her eyes and burnt her roses.

I offered her a cup. . . .

And came to paradise. . . .

Ah, sorrow,
When she rose from the waves of wine
I thought she would have killed me
With the swords of her desolation. . . .

Especially as I had tied her girdle
With the wrong bow.

From the Arabic of Abu Nuas (8th Century).

AN ESCAPE

She was beautiful that evening and so gay. . . .

In little games
My hand had slipped her mantle,
I am not sure
About her skirts.

Then in the night's curtain of shadows,
Heavy and discreet,
I asked and she replied:
To-morrow.

57

Next day I came
Saying, Remember.

Words of a night, she said, to bring the day.
From the Arabic of Abu Nuas (8th Century).

THREE QUEENS

Three sweet drivers hold the reins,
And hold the places of my heart.
A great people obeys me,
But these three obey me not.
Am I then a lesser king than love?
From the Arabic of Haroun El Rashid
(8th Century).

PERTURBATION AT DAWN

Day comes. . . .

And when she sees the withering of the violet garden
And the saffron garden flowering,
The stars escaping on their black horse
And dawn on her white horse arriving,
She is afraid.

Against the sighing of her frightened breasts
She puts her hand;
I see what I have never seen,
Five perfect lines on a crystal leaf
Written with coral pens.
From the Arabic of Ebn Maatuk (17th Century).

MOALLAKA

The poets have muddied all the little fountains.

Yet do not my strong eyes know you, far house?

O dwelling of Abla in the valley of Gawa,
Speak to me, for my camel and I salute you.

My camel is as tall as a tower, and I make him stand
And give my aching heart to the wind of the desert.

O erstwhile dwelling of Abla in the valley of Gawa;
And my tribe in the valleys of Hazn and Samna
And in the valley of Motethalem!

Salute to the old ruins, the lonely ruins
Since Oum El Aythan gathered and went away.

Now is the dwelling of Abla
In a valley of men who roar like lions.
It will be hard to come to you, O daughter of Makh-
ram.

. . . .

Abla is a green rush
That feeds beside the water.

But they have taken her to Oneiza
And my tribe feeds in lazy Ghailam valley.

They fixed the going, and the camels
Waked in the night and evilly prepared.

I was afraid when I saw the camels
Standing ready among the tents
And eating grain to make them swift.

I counted forty-two milk camels,
Black as the wings of a black crow.

White and purple are the lilies of the valley,
But Abla is a branch of flowers.

Who will guide me to the dwelling of Abla?

From the Arabic of Antar
(late 6th and early 7th Centuries).

MOALLAKA

Rise and hold up the curved glass,
And pour us wine of the morning, of El Andar.

Pour wine for us, whose golden colour
Is like a water stream kissing flowers of saffron.

Pour us wine to make us generous
And carelessly happy in the old way.

Pour us wine that gives the miser
A sumptuous generosity and disregard.

O Um-Amr, you have prevented me from the cup
When it should have been moving to the right;
And yet the one of us three that you would not serve
Is not the least worthy.

How many cups have I not emptied at Balbek,
And emptied at Damas and emptied at Cacerin!

More cups! more cups! for death will have his day;
His are we and he ours.

    •   •   •   •

By herself she is fearless
And gives her arms to the air,
The limbs of a long camel that has not borne.

She gives the air her breasts,
Unfingered ivory.

She gives the air her long self and her curved self,
And hips so round and heavy that they are tired.

All these noble abundances of girlhood
Make the doors divinely narrow and myself insane.

Columns of marble and ivory in the old way,
And anklets chinking in gold and musical bracelets.

Without her I am a she-camel that has lost,
And howls in the sand at night.

Without her I am as sad as an old mother
Hearing of the death of her many sons.

From the Arabic of Amr Ebn Kultum
(7th Century).

A CANKER IN THE HEART

I made a bitter song
When I was a boy,
About a girl
With hot earth-coloured hair,
Who lived with me
And left me.

I made a sour song
On her marriage-day,
That ever his kisses
Would be ghosts of mine,
And ever the measure
Of his halting love
Flow to my music.

It was a silly song,
Dear wife with cool black hair,
And yet when I recall
(At night with you asleep)
That once you gave yourself
Before we met,
I do not quite well know
What song to make.

From the Burmese
(*19th Century*) (*? by Asmapur*).

VENGEANCE

Aischa was mine,
My tender cousin,
My blond lover;
And you knew our love,
Uncle without bowels,
Foul old man.

For a few weights of gold
You sold her to the blacks,
And they will drive a stinking trade
At the dark market;
Your slender daughter,
The free child of our hills.

She will go to serve the bed
Of a fat man with no god,
A guts that cannot walk,
A belly hiding his own feet,
A rolling paunch
Between itself and love.

She was slim and quick
Like the antelope of our hills
When he comes down in the summer-time
To bathe in the pools of Terek,
Her stainless flesh
Was all moonlight.

Her long silk hair
Was of so fine a gold
And of so honey-like a brown
That bees flew there,
And her red lips
Were flowers in sunlight.

She was fair, alas, she was fair,
So that her beauty goes
To a garden of dying flowers,
Made one with the girls that mourn
And wither for light and love
Behind the harem bars.

And you have dirty dreams
That she will be Sultane,
And you will drink and boast
And roll about,
The grinning ancestor
Of little kings.

Hugging your very wicked gold
Within a greasy belt,
You paddle exulting like a bald ape
That glories to defile,
Unmindful of two hot young streams
Of tears.

You stole this dirty gold,
For this gold means
Your daughter's freedom
And your nephew's love,
Two fresh and lovely things
Groaning within your belt.

The sunny playing of our childhood
At the green foot of Elbrus,
The starry playing of our youth
Beyond the flowery fences,
These sigh their lost delights
Within your belt.

Give me the gold;
Damn you, give me the gold. . . .
You kill my mercy
When you kill my love. . . .
Hold up your trembling sword;
For this is death.

* * * *

I take the belt from the dead loins
That put away my love,
And turn my sweet white horse
After the caravan. . . .
With dirty gold and clean steel
I'll set Aischa free.

Ballad of the Caucasus.

WE WERE TWO GREEN RUSHES

We were two green rushes by opposing banks,
    And the small stream ran between.
Not till the water beat us down
    Could we be brought together,
Not till the winter came
Could we be mingled in a frosty sleep,
    Locked down and close.

From the Chinese of J. Wing (19th Century).

SONG WRITER PAID WITH AIR

I sit on a white wood box
Smeared with the black name
Of a seller of white sugar.
The little brown table is so dirty
That if I had food
I do not think I could eat.

How can I promise violets drunken in wine
For your amusement,
How can I powder your blue cotton dress
With splinters of emerald,
How can I sing you songs of the amber pear,
Or pour for the finger-tips of your white fingers
Mingled scents in a rose agate bowl?

From the Chinese of J. Wing (19th Century).

THE BAD ROAD

I have seen a pathway shaded by green great trees,
A road bordered by thickets light with flowers.

My eyes have entered in under the green shadow,
And made a cool journey far along the road.

But I shall not take the road,
Because it does not lead to her house.

When she was born
They shut her little feet in iron boxes,
So that my belovèd never walks the roads.

When she was born
They shut her heart in a box of iron,
So that my belovèd shall never love me.

From the Chinese.

THE WESTERN WINDOW

At the head of a thousand roaring warriors,
With the sound of gongs,
My husband has departed
Following glory.

At first I was overjoyed
To have a young girl's liberty.

Now I look at the yellowing willow-leaves;
They were green the day he left.

I wonder if he also was glad?

From the Chinese of Wang Ch'ang Ling
(8th Century).

THE WILLOW-LEAF

I am in love with a child dreaming at the window.

Not for her elaborate house
On the banks of Yellow River;

But for a willow-leaf she has let fall
    Into the water.

I am in love with the east breeze.

Not that he brings the scent of the flowering of peaches
    White on Eastern Hill;

But that he has drifted the willow-leaf
   Against my boat.

I am in love with the willow-leaf.

Not that he speaks of green spring
   Coming to us again;

But that the dreaming girl
Pricked there a name with her embroidery needle,
   And the name is mine.

From the Chinese of Chang Chiu Ling (675-740).

THE JADE STAIRCASE

The jade staircase is bright with dew.

Slowly, this long night, the queen climbs,
   Letting her gauze stockings and her elaborate robe
Drag in the shining water.

Dazed with the light,
She lowers the crystal blind
Before the door of the pavilion.

It leaps down like a waterfall in sunlight.

While the tiny clashing dies down,
Sad and long dreaming,
She watches between the fragments of jade light
The shining of the autumn moon.

From the Chinese of Li Po (705-762).

WRITTEN ON A WALL IN SPRING

It rained last night,
But fair weather has come back
This morning.

The green clusters of the palm trees
Open and begin to throw shadows.

But sorrow drifts slowly down about me.

I come and go in my room,
Heart-heavy with memories.

The neighbour green casts shadows of green
On my blind;
The moss, soaked in dew,
Takes the least print
Like delicate velvet.

I see again a gauze tunic of oranged rose
With shadowy underclothes of grenade red.

How things still live again.

I go and sit by the day balustrade

And do nothing

Except count the plains
And the mountains
And the valleys
And the rivers
That separate from my Spring.

From the Chinese (early 19*th Century).*

IN THE COLD NIGHT

Reading in my book this cold night,
I have forgotten to go to sleep.
The perfumes have died on the gilded bed-cover;
The last smoke must have left the hearth
When I was not looking .
My beautiful friend snatches away the lamp.
Do you know what the time is?

From the Chinese of Yuan Mei (1715-1797).

FARD

Love brings the tiny sweat into your hair
Like stars marching in the dead of night.

From the Hindustani of Mir Taqui
(18th Century).

FARD

Ever your rose face or black curls are with Shaguil;
Because your curls are night and your face is day.

From the Hindustani of Shaguil
(18th Century).

DRINK SONG

The crows have wakened me
By cawing at the moon.
I pray that I shall not think of him;
I pray so intently
That he begins to fill my whole mind.
This is getting on my nerves;
I wonder if there is any of that wine left.

Japanese Street Song.

70

THE OPINION OF MEN

My desires are like the white snows on Fuji
That grow but never melt.
I am becoming proud of my bad reputation;
And the more men say,
We cannot understand why she loves him,
The less I care.
I am sure that in a very short time
I shall give myself to him.

Japanese Street Song.

AN ORANGE SLEEVE

In the fifth month,
When orange-trees
Fill all the world with scent,
I think of the sleeve
Of a girl who loved me.

From the Japanese of Nari-hira.

GREEN FOOD FOR A QUEEN

I was gathering
Leaves of the Wakana
In springtime.
Why did the snow fall
On my dress?

From the Japanese of the Mikado
Ko-ko Ten-no (9th Century).

THE CUSHION

Your arm should only be
A spring night's dream;
If I accepted it to rest my head upon
There would be rumours
And no delight.

From the Japanese of the daughter of
Taira-no Tsu-gu-naka.

A SINGLE NIGHT

Was one night,
And that a night
Without much sleep,
Enough to make me love
All the life long?

From the Japanese of the wife of the
Mikado Sui-toku In (12th Century).

PROPOSAL OF MARRIAGE

Your eyes are black like water-melon pips,
Your lips are red like the red flesh of water-melons,
Your loins are smooth like smooth-rind water-melons.

You are more beautiful than my favourite among
   mares,
Your buttocks are sleeker and firmer,
Like her your movements are on legs of light steel.

72

Come and sit at my hearth, and I will celebrate your
    coming;
I will choose from the hundred flocks of each a hun-
    dred,
Passing at the foot of the Himalaya,

The two most silky and most beautiful great sheep.
We will go to the temple and sacrifice one of the two
To the god Pandu, that you may have many children;

And I will kill the other and roast it whole,
My most fair rose-tree serving as a spit.
I will ask the prettiest eaters and the prettiest drinkers;

And while they eat and drink greatly for three days,
I will wind silver rings upon your arms and feet
And hang a chain of river gold about your neck.
                              Popular Song of Kafiristan.

TEARS

How can a heart play any more with life,
    After it has found a woman and known tears?

In vain I shut my windows against the moonlight;
    I have estranged sleep.

The flower of her face is growing in the shadow
    Among warm and rustling leaves. . . .

I see the sunlight on her house,
I see her curtains of vermilion silk. . . .

Here is the almond-coloured dawn;
And there is dew on the petals of my night flower.
Lyric of Korea.

PARADISE

Paradise, my darling, know that paradise,
The Prophet-given paradise after death,
Is far and very mysterious and most high;
My habits would be upset in such a place.

Without impiety, I should be mortally weary
If I went there alone, without my wife;
An ugly crowding of inferior females,
What should I do with the houris?

What should I do with those tall loaded fruit-trees,
Seeing I could not give the fruit to you?
What by the freshness of those blue streams,
Seeing my face reflected there alone?

And it might be worse if you came with me,
For all of Allah's Chosen would desire you.
And if Mahomet threw his handkerchief
And took you up and loved you for himself?

Eyes of my eyes, how could I then defend you?
I could not be at ease and watch him love you;
And if I mutinied against the Prophet,
He, being zealous to love you in his peace,

74

Would rise and send me hurrying
Back by the sword-blade thinness of the bridge
From paradise to earth, and in the middle
Flick me down sideways to the fires of hell.

My skin would cook and be renewed for ever
Where murderers were burning and renewing;
And evil souls, my only crime being love,
Would burn me and annoy me and destroy me.

If I were there and you in paradise,
I could not even make my prayer to Allah
That in his justice he should give me back
My paradise.

Let us love, therefore, on the earth together;
Our love is our garden, let us take great care,
Whisper and call pet names and kiss each other
To live our paradise as long as may be.

Love Ballad of Kurdistan.

KHAP-SALUNG

Seeing that I adore you,
Scarf of golden flowers,
Why do you stay unmarried?
As the liana at a tree's foot
That quivers to wind it round,
So do I wait for you. I pray you
Do not detest me. . . .

I have come to say farewell.
Farewell, scarf;
Garden Royal
Where none may enter,
Gaudy money
I may not spend.

Song of the Love Nights of Laos.

THE HOLY SWAN

Fair journey, O holy swan with gold wings;
O holy swan that I love, fair journey!
Carry this letter for me to the new land,
The place where my lover labours.
If it rains fly low beneath the trees,
If the sun is hot fly in the forest shadows;
If any ask you where you are going
Do not answer.
You who rise for so long a journey,
Avoid the roofs at the hour when the sun is red.
Carry this letter to the new land of my lover.
If he is faithful, give it to him;
If he has forgotten, read it to him only
And let the lightning burn it afterwards.

Song of the Love Nights of Laos.

TOO SHORT A NIGHT

Lily of Streams lay by my side last night
And to my prayers gave answers of delight;
Day came before our fairy-tale was finished,
Because the tale was long, not short the night.

*From the Persian of Abu-Said
(978-1062).*

76

SEE YOU HAVE DANCERS

See you have dancers and wine and a girl like one of
  the angels
          (If they exist),
And find a clear stream singing near its birth and a
  bed of moss
          (If moss exists),
For loving and singing to the dancers and drinking
  and forgetting hell
          (If hell exists),
Because this is a pastime better than paradise
          (If paradise exists).

From the Persian of Omar Khayyám
(11th Century).

THE SIGHING HEART

I made search for you all my life, and when I found
  you
There came a trouble on me,
So that it seemed my blood escaped
And my life ran back from me
And my heart slipped into you.
It seems, also, that you are the moon
And that I am at the top of a tree.
If I had wings I would spread them as far as you,
Dear bud, that will not open
Though the kisses of the holy bird knock at your petal
  door.

Song of Siam.

THE LOVE OF THE ARCHER PRINCE

The Khan.

The son of the Khan.

The love of the son of the Khan.

The veil of the love of the son of the Khan.

The clear breeze that lifted the veil of the love of the
son of the Khan.

The buds of fire that scented the clear breeze that
lifted the veil of the love of the son of the Khan.

The Archer Prince whose love kissed the buds of fire
that scented the clear breeze that lifted the veil of
the love of the son of the Khan.

And the girl married the Archer Prince whose love
kissed the buds of fire that scented the clear breeze
that lifted the veil of the love of the son of the Khan.

Street Song of Thibet.

A PROVERB

Before you love,
Learn to run through snow
Leaving no footprint.

From the Turkish.

ENVOY IN AUTUMN

Here are the doleful rains,
And one would say the sky is weeping
The death of the tolerable weather.

Tedium cloaks the wit like a veil of clouds
And we sit down indoors.

Now is the time for poetry coloured with summer.
Let it fall on the white paper
As ripe flowers fall from a perfect tree.

I will dip down my lips into my cup
Each time I wet my brush.

And keep my thoughts from wandering as smoke
   wanders,
For time escapes away from you and me
Quicker than birds.

From the Chinese of Tu Fu (712-770).

NOTES.

If readers care to turn to *Anthologie de l'Amour Asiatique*, compiled by Adolphe Thalasso ... they will find a full and clear study of Asia's love poetry and see how much I owe to this erudite and stimulating authority. M. Thalasso's work first showed me beauty and interest in the songs of almost unknown literatures. In some instances I have translated directly and only from his book, in others I have gratefully taken his direction and traced poems back to their sources. Versions also, of some of the Chinese poems given here will be found in the incomparable *"Livre de Jade of* Mme Judith Gautier." Reference to texts of other poems is easily made at various libraries, except with regard to a dozen which I have personally collected. These last have not before, I think, been given a European form.

Black Hair. For many of the forty years of his life, which closed in madness in 1890, Muhammadji, the greatest poet of Afghanistan, was working out sentences in prison for violent brawling and heavy drinking. In the last stanza of this poem the folly of grandeurs is easily detected; and in all his work, mingled with that drowsy music which was his greatness, is a vertigo from over the depths of insanity.

BLACK MARIGOLDS

Nineteen hundred years ago, when Bhartrihari was writing, Chauras, a young Brahman poet, lived at the Court of King Sundava in Kanchinpur, and loved Vidya, the king's daughter. It is said that on the discovery of their love Chauras was imprisoned and executed; and that it was in the last few hours of his life that he composed his love lament, the *Chaurapanchasika*: "the Fifty Stanzas of Chauras."

Though the poem which is printed here has verses of direct, almost literal, translation, it would be fairer to Chauras to consider it, in its entirety, as an interpretation rather than as a translation of his work; an attempt to bring over into an English poem the spirit of mournful exaltation which informs his Sanskrit leavetaking.

I have tried to imitate the abrupt rise from earth which his poem makes about the fifteenth stanza; and I have also tried, by not letting my verse become a coherent lyric poem in the English sense, to keep his disjointed air, as of a set-form sequence, in which the stanzas are bound together only by a thread of feeling. Asia knows nothing of the long lyric, save in that sense which could describe Rossetti's "House of Life" or Shakespeare's Sonnets.

The first "shloke" of each stanza in the original starts with *adyapi*, a word of reminiscence, and this gives to the poem a recurring monotone of retrospection, which I hope my unchanging *Even now* also suggests.

My rendering was finished in 1915, in two or three sessions on a box by the stove in hutments; and I have not cared to risk a discrepancy of moods in more luxurious minutes and places.

RAHU, an evil spirit, half man and half snake, who swallowed the sun and the moon at times of eclipse.

RATI, is desire, the bride of love.

TIRTHA, an artificial lake filled with sacred water.

GARDEN OF BRIGHT WATERS

I am hoping that some readers will look on this collection primarily as a book of poems. The finding and selection of material and the shaping of the verses is my principal part in it. Most of the songs have been written from, or by comparing, the literal translations of French and Italian scholars, checked wherever possible by my own knowledge. When my first and very great debt to these has been stated, there remains my debt to the late John Duncan, to Mr. J. Wing, and to a friend, a distinguished writer both in Persian and Turkish, who wishes to remain unnamed. The kindness of these writers lies in trusting their work to my translation and helping me in that task. My book also owes much to suggestions prompted by the wide learning of Mr. L. Cranmer-Byng. My final debt is to him and to another generous critic. I have arranged my poems in the alphabetical order of their countries, and added short notes wherever I considered them necessary, at the instance of some kindly reviewers of an earlier book, which was not so arranged and provided.

AFGHANISTAN

SIKANDER, Alexander the Great.

SHALIBAGH, the notable garden of Shalimar in Lahore, planted by Shah Jahan in 1637.

ABDEL QADIR GILANI, Abd al-Qadir al-Jilani, founder of the Qadirite order of the Dervishes, twelfth century.

ANNAM

K'IEN NIÜ and CHIK NÜ: the legend of these two stars comes from China and is told in Japan. Readers are referred to that section of Mr. L. Cranmer-Byng's *A Lute of Jade* which deals delightfully with Po-Chü-i; and to Lafcadio Hearn's *Romance of the Milky Way*.

ARABIC

ANTAR, the hero Antar Ebn Cheddad Ebn Amr Corad, who lived in the late sixth and early seventh centuries, owes his European reputation to *Siret Antar*, the Adventures of Antar, or more exactly the Conduct of Antar, written by Abul-Moyyed "El Antari" in the twelfth century. This book tells of the fighter's feats in war and of his love for his cousin Abla; and these are the themes of Antar's own poems.

An Escape: in this poem Abu Nuas, the Court poet, tells of an adventure of the Khalif Haroun. There is a story that the Khalif, being set back by the answer of his lady, called his poets in the morning and bade them write a poem round the phrase, "Words of a night to bring the day". All were rewarded for their work save Abu Nuas; and he was condemned to death for spying through keyholes on his master. But after he had proved an alibi, he also was rewarded.

JAPAN

WAKANA, the turnip cabbage, whose leaves are eaten in early spring. The Mikado is lamenting a sudden realization that he is too old for his love.

The Cushion: the poetess, daughter of Tsu-gunaka, lord of Su-Wo, while at a party, asked for a cushion. A certain Iye-tada offered his arm for her to lean her head against, and she answered with these lines.

STREET SONGS: the three poems which I have so called are written in everyday colloquial Japanese. The words of the old language, which are the ornament of literary verse, are almost entirely excluded from these songs. In them one finds a superabundance of auxiliaries, and the presence of these marks a clear line between the literary and the folk-idiom.

LAOS

THE LOVE NIGHTS OF LAOS, "Wan-Pak" Nights, at the eighth evening of the waxing or waning of the moon, when even Buddha has no fault to find with love-making in the thickets. Songs, of which I have translated three, are sung on these nights to the accompaniment of the "Khane", a pan-pipe of seven flutes; some being reserved for the singing of the wandering bands of girls, and others for answer by the youths.

THIBET

The Love of the Archer Prince: this form of poem, with one rhyme and repetitive and increasing lines, is a familiar one in Thibet; and thence it has entered Kafiristan and become a popular manner of composition there. There are folk-chants in this form current in the Grecian Archipelago. English readers will remember an analogous poem. *The House that Jack built.*

CHISWICK PRESS

TORQUEMADA—(POWYS MATHERS)
112 BEST CROSSWORD PUZZLES

Manchester Evening News.—"If there was a 'Crossword King' it was Torquemada."

With 3 Biographical Notes of the man, the poet, and the translator. Portrait. 390 pp. **9/.**

EVGENY ONEGIN—PUSHKIN

Translated: OLIVER ELTON; Decorations: M. V. DOBUJINSKY; Foreword: DESMOND MACCARTHY. 290 pp. **9/.**

Manchester Guardian.—"This brilliant and fluid rendering."

The Times Literary Supplement.—"Pushkin in Russian Poetry is what Shakespeare is in English."

DISTANT POINT—AFINOGENEV

Translated by HUBERT GRIFFITH. **2/6**

PRESS NOTICES

Daily Herald.—"Russia's best play."

Yorkshire Evening Post.—"No better play from Soviet Russia has reached this country."

FORM OF DIARY—ANON

A remarkable ultra-modern psychological document. 444 pp. **7/6**

To the Author, long before this book was written, GEORGE BERNARD SHAW wrote:—"*You have a talent which is more irresistible than Shelley's and Tolstoy's rolled together . . . you will be one of the greatest of English women writers, in fact one of the greatest of all English writers before you are thirty-three.*"

TOPSY: THE STORY OF A CHOW
MARIE BONAPARTE

Indication of the enduring worth of this unusual dog story is the fact that the German translation was made by SIGM. and ANNA FREUD.

With 8 Illustrations. **7/6**

AN ADDER'S NEST—V. LEVSTIK

A Slovene classic: An inspired call to freedom, to individual and national emancipation. A story of Slovene peasant life under the German jackboot. With 4 Illustrations. **7/6**

Observer.—"A remarkable novel . . ."